More *Permission Granted*

Don Byrd and Leanna Wolfe

Published by LONGSTREET PRESS, INC.,
a subsidiary of Cox Newspapers, a subsidiary of Cox Enterprises, Inc.
2140 Newmarket Parkway, Suite 118
Marietta, Georgia 30067

Copyright © 1995 by Don Byrd and Leanna Wolfe

All rights reserved. No part of this book may be reproduced in any form by any means without the prior written permission of the Publisher, excepting brief quotations used in connection with reviews, written specifically for inclusion in a magazine or newspaper.

Printed in the United States of America

1st revised printing, 1995
This book was previously published by Longstreet Press under a different title.

ISBN: 1-56352-318-3

Book and cover design by Jill Dible

More Permission Granted

More Permission Granted begins where *Permission Granted* left off. Again, you are invited to explore new frontiers, honor differences, laugh, and grow closer. Now you can tell a whole story without being interrupted, star in your own X-rated video, gain full charge of the remote control (limited time only!), receive kisses someplace very private, put an immediate end to over-analyzing, indulge in a no-limits massage, or escape into a no-questions-asked internet adventure. *More Permission Granted* can help to energize your relationship if you:

- Keep them in a special place and open them up for communication emergencies, to charge up a potentially dull sex life, and to escape…
- Carry them in your purse or bag to use everyday for permissions, exploration, intimacy, and fun!

How to Use *More Permission Granted*

More Permission Granted can be enjoyed by:

- Giving them as a gift to your partner and then inviting him/her to redeem them with you as desired. Once redeemed, coupons can be recycled to further the exchange…
- Receiving them as a couple's gift to share together, allowing each of you take turns giving and receiving…

Soon you may find the permissions, negotiations, and adventure that *More Permission Granted* invite will become so much a part of you relationship, you won't need an actual coupon to express what you desire. Until then, enjoy…

XXX COUPON

Redeemable For

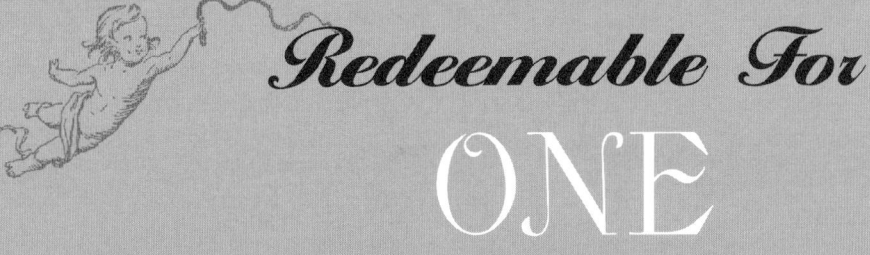

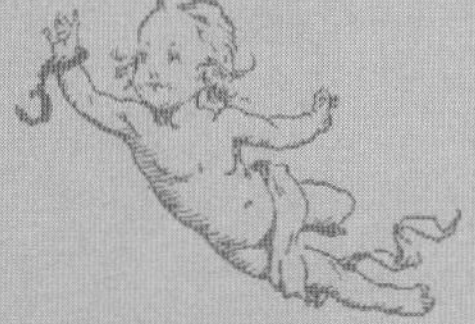

ONE

Private Strip Tease

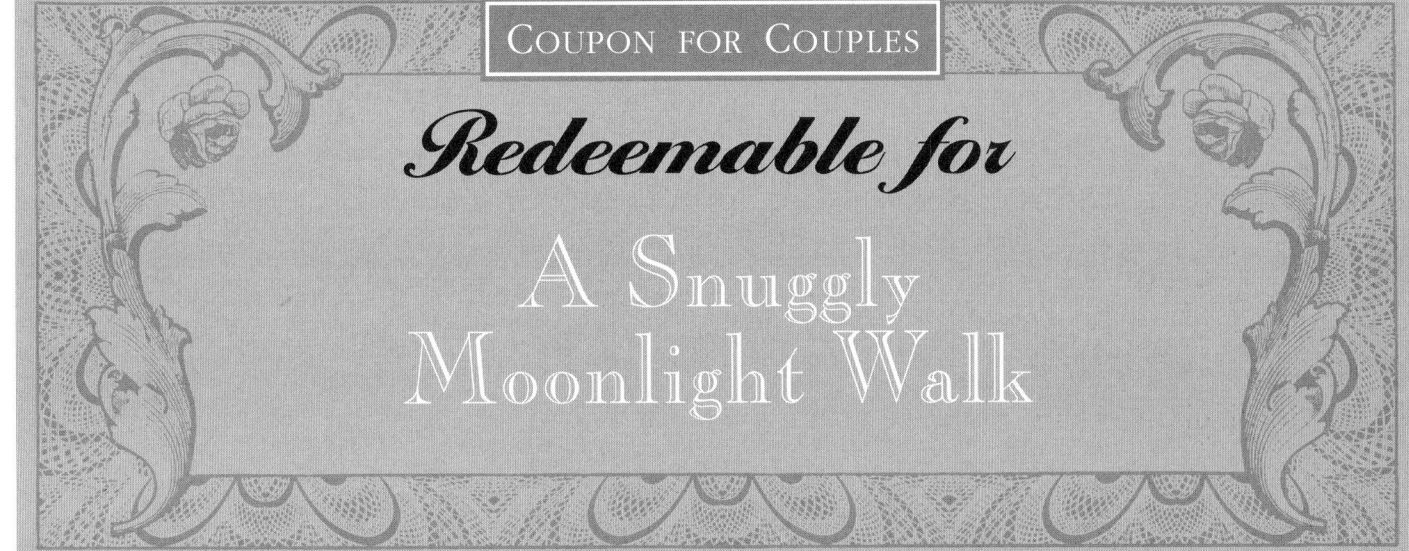

XXX COUPON

Invites Bearer to

Try a New Position

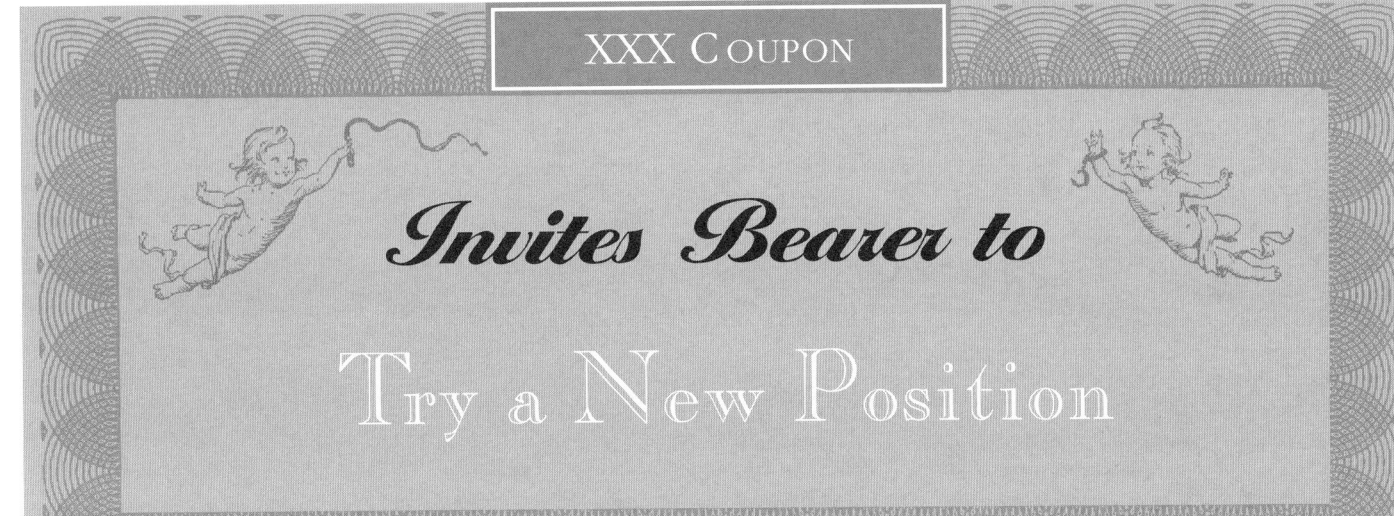

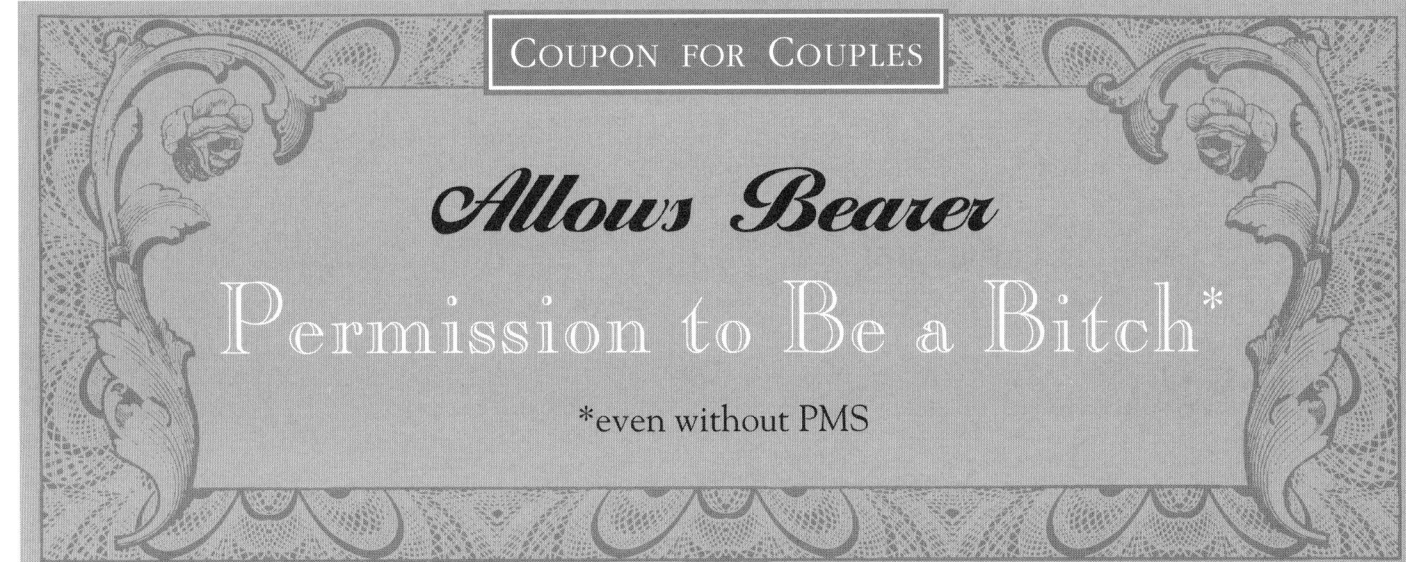

XXX Coupon

Redeemable For
A Dangerous Liaison Fantasy

XXX Coupon

Guarantees

Kisses in a Private Place*

*You Decide!

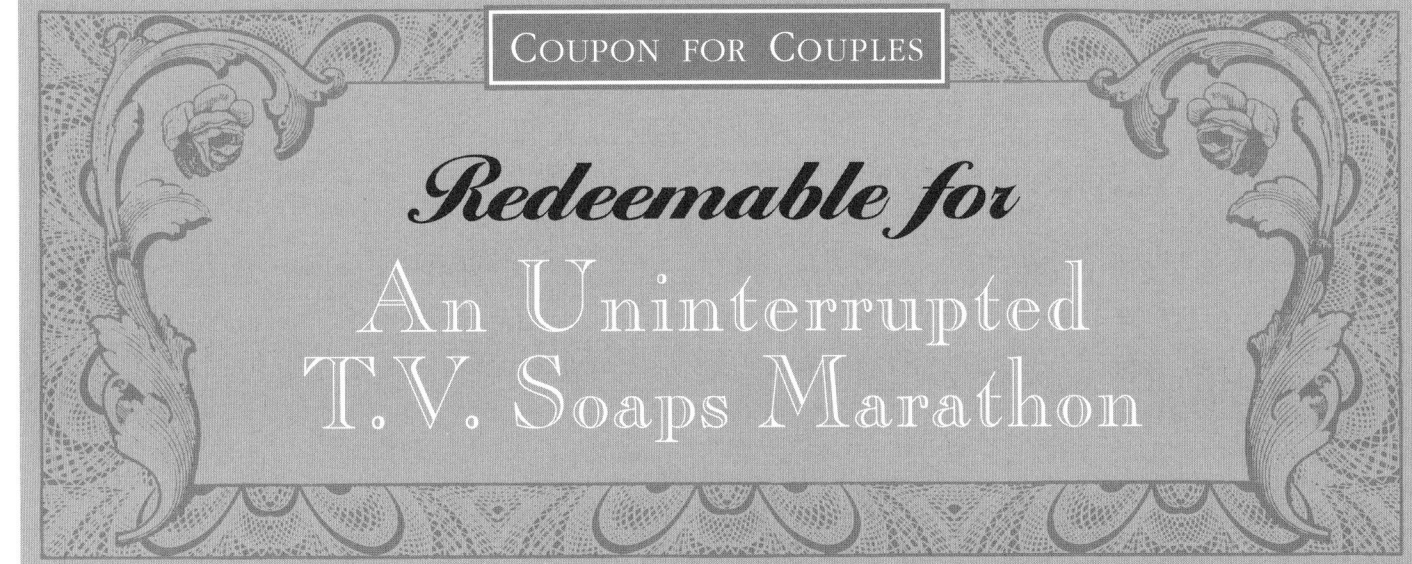

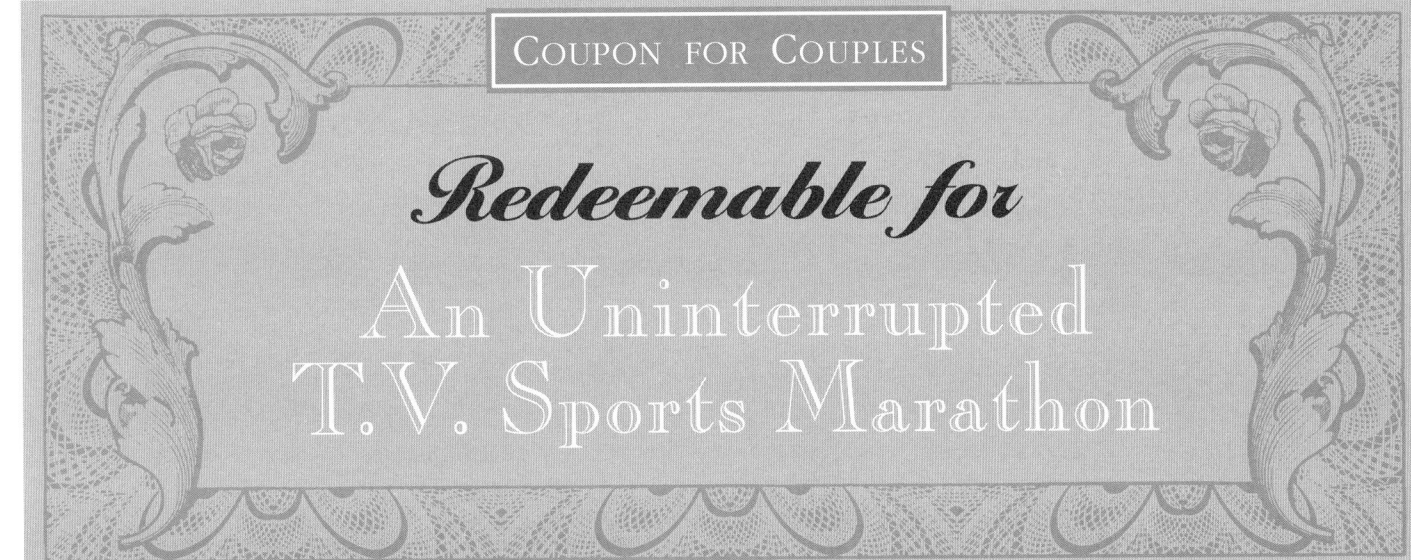

XXX Coupon

Invites Bearer To Play Doctor

*full examination expected!

COUPON FOR COUPLES

Guarantees Permission

To Tell Your Version of the Story*

*no interruptions!

XXX Coupon

Guarantees Bearer

Sex Someplace New*

*not the bedroom

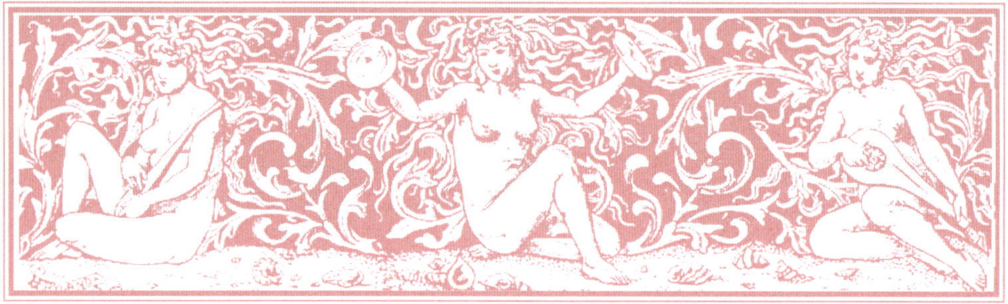

Coupon for Couples

Guarantees Bearer

Full Charge of the Remote Control*

*limited time only!

Coupon for Couples

Allows Bearer

A Totally Private Weekend*

*no phones, beepers, faxes, or e-mail

XXX Coupon

Allows Bearer

Starring Role
In X-rated Home Video

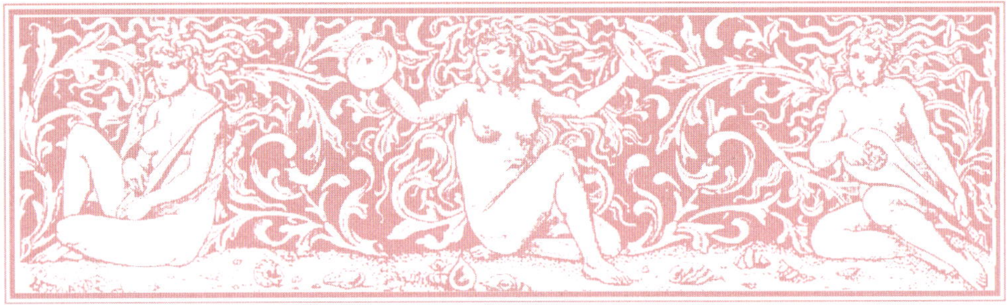

XXX Coupon

Allows Bearer

To Direct X-rated Home Video*

*I'll be the star…

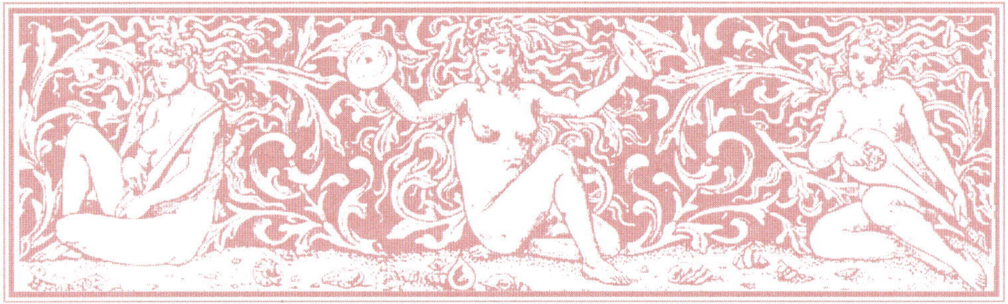

XXX Coupon

Guarantees

ONE

Crotchless Panties Night Out

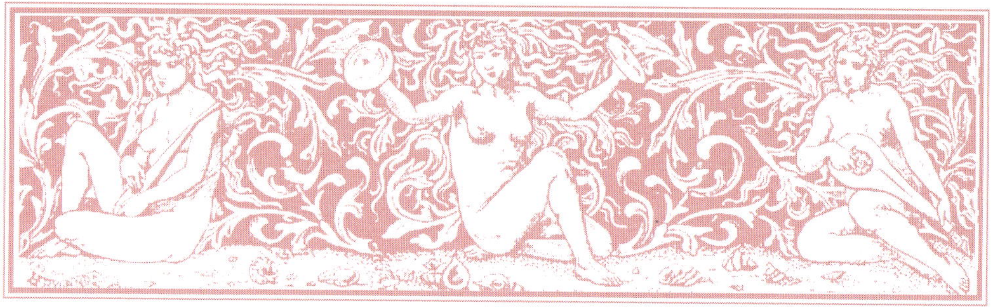

Coupon for Couples

Guarantees

A Little Tickling*

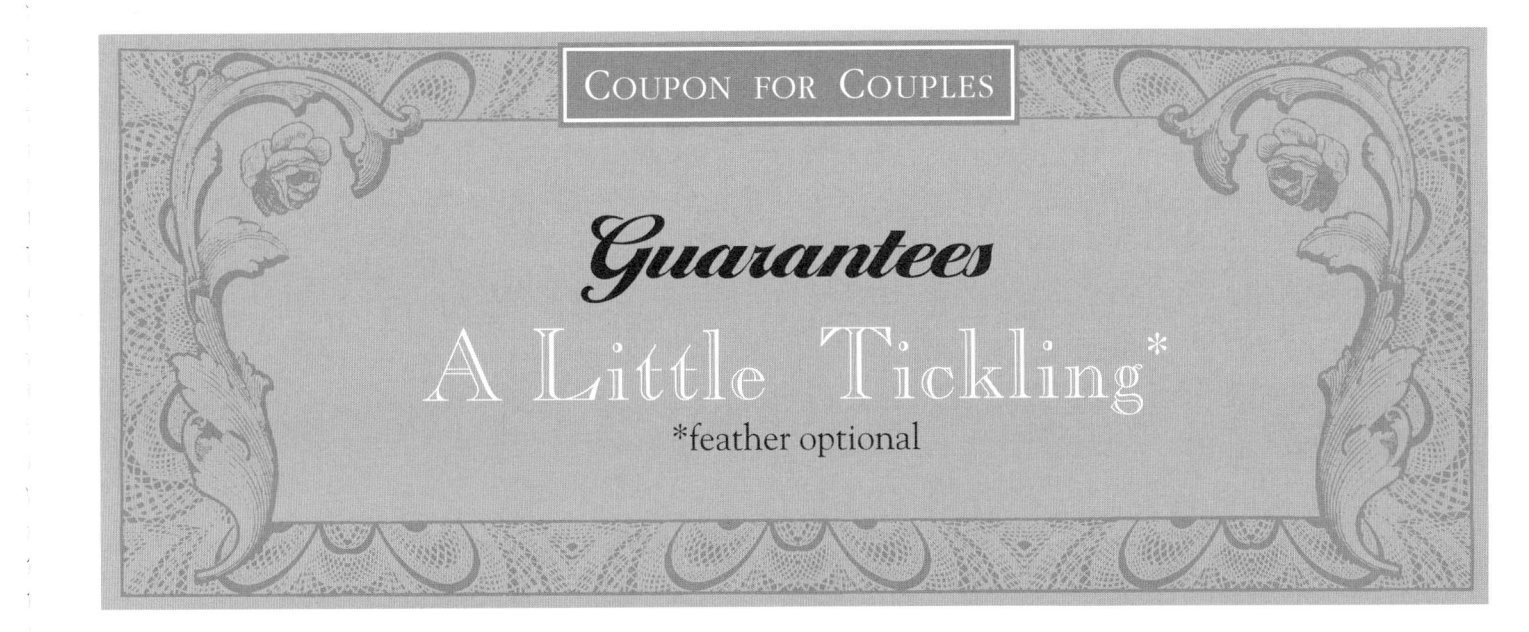

*feather optional

XXX Coupon

Allows Bearer

A Blindfold and/or Handcuffs Adventure

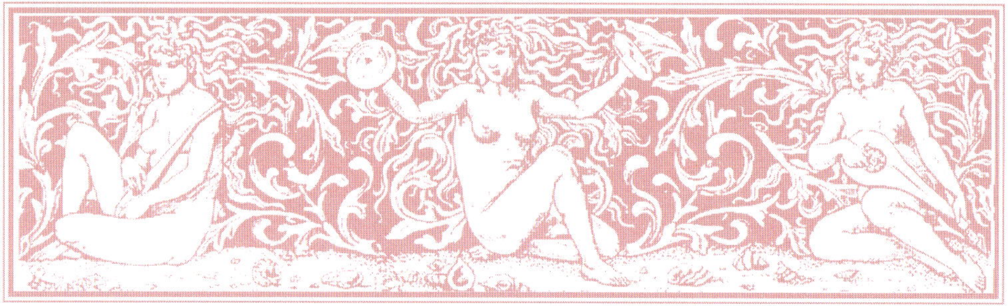

XXX Coupon

Allows Bearer

ONE

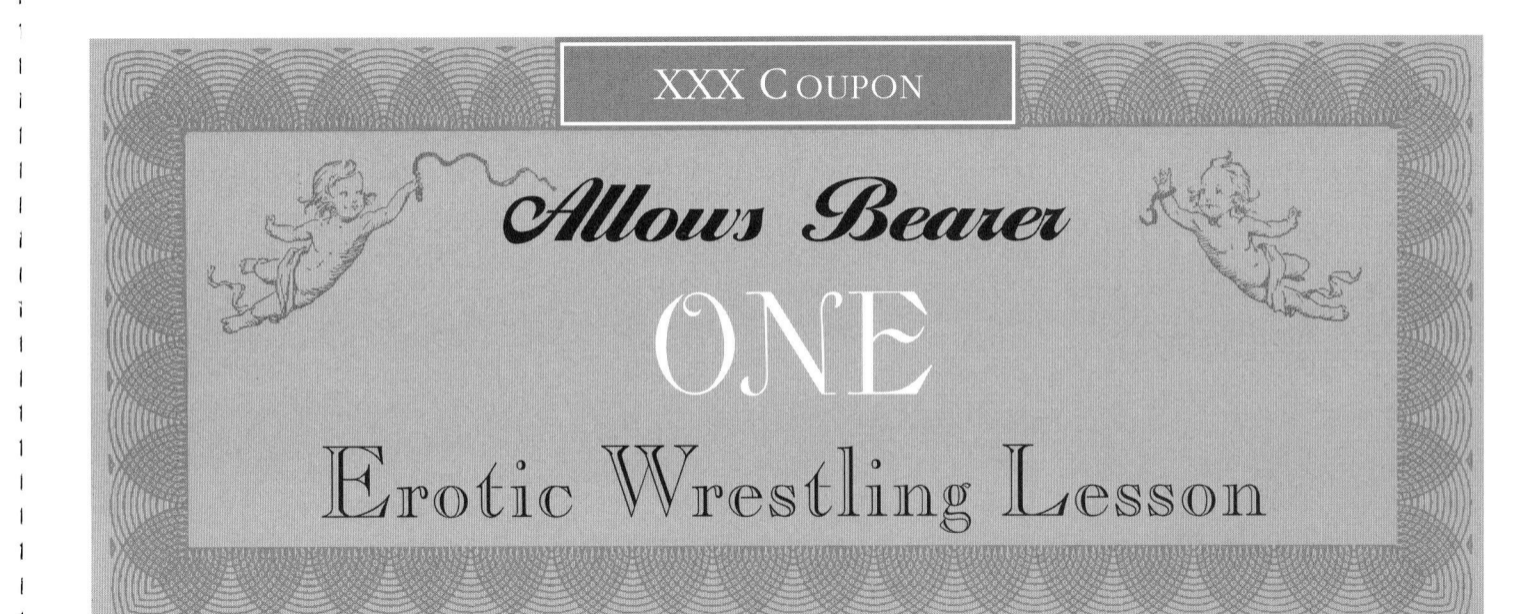

Erotic Wrestling Lesson

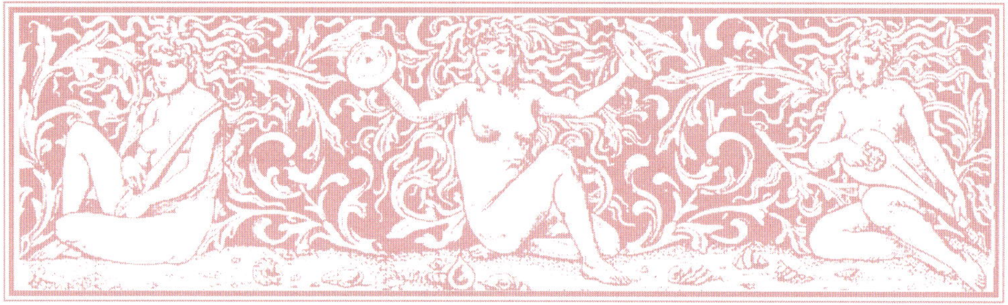

Coupon for Couples

Allows Bearer

Immediate End to Over-Analyzing

XXX Coupon

Allows Bearer
ONE
Full Submission Evening*
*collar and leash optional

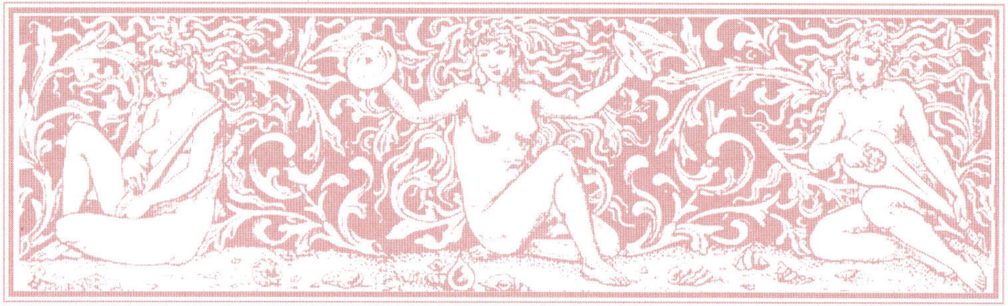

Coupon for Couples

Allows Bearer

ONE HOUR

No-Objections Help

XXX Coupon

Redeemable For
An Uninterrupted X-rated Video Marathon

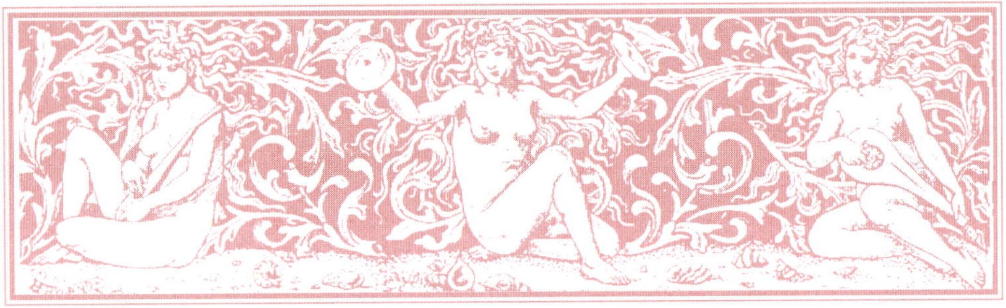

XXX Coupon

Guarantees Permission
To Talk Dirty*

*just to me…

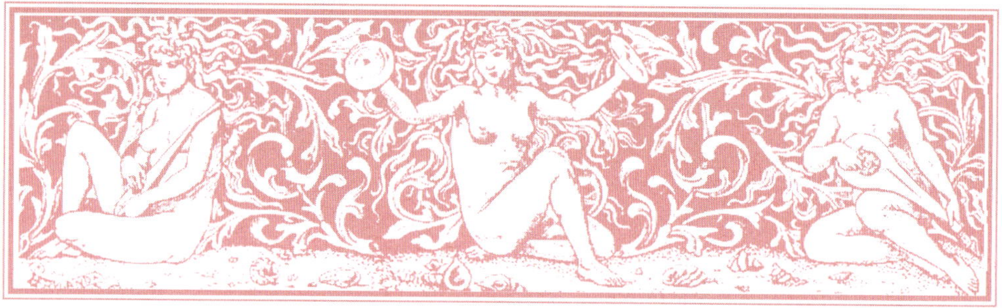

COUPON FOR COUPLES

Allows Bearer

ONE

Four Hands Massage

XXX Coupon

Redeemable For
ONE
Ménage à Trois*

*or more

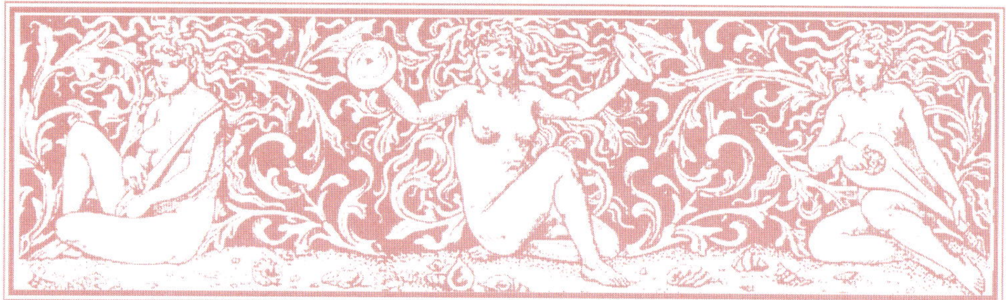

Coupon for Couples

Allows Bearer Permission

To Be Grumpy*

*and look it too!

XXX Coupon

Entitles Bearer To

Play Strip Poker*

*with players of choice

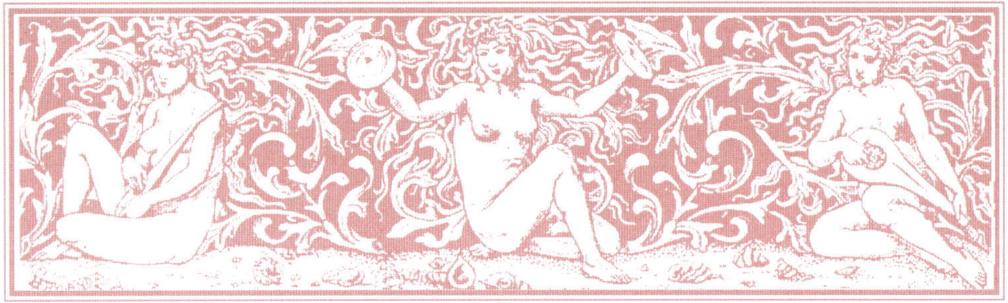

Coupon for Couples

Grants Permission
To Back-Seat Drive

COUPON FOR COUPLES

Redeemable For

ONE

Leave-Me-Alone Day

XXX Coupon

Allows Bearer

ONE

No Limits Massage*

*no parts untouched

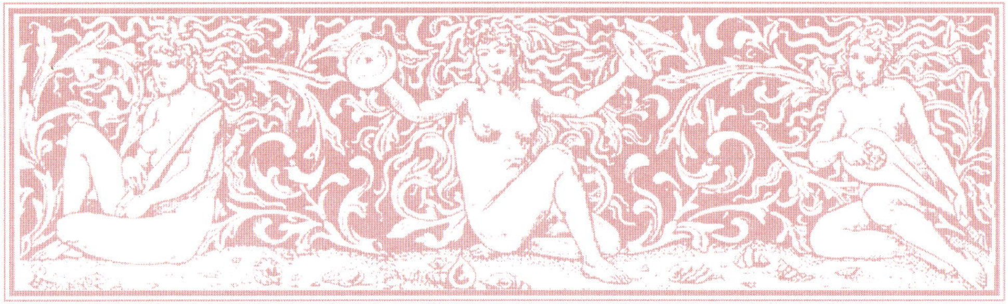

XXX Coupon

Allows Bearer
ONE
No Limits Massage*
*no parts untouched

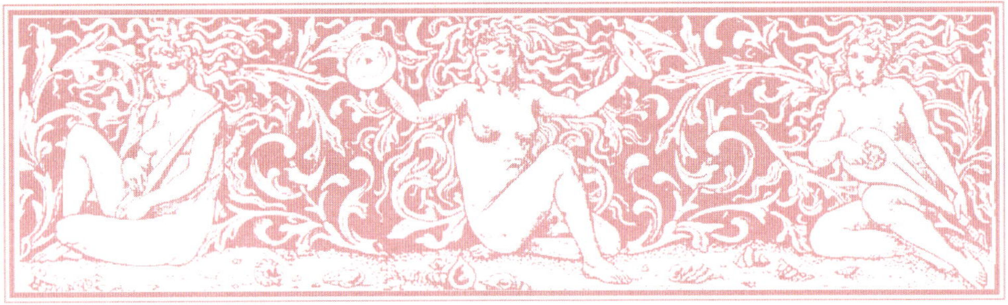

COUPON FOR COUPLES

Redeemable For

A Slow-Dance Evening*

*you pick the music…

Coupon for Couples

Allows Bearer

To Get Lost in the Woods

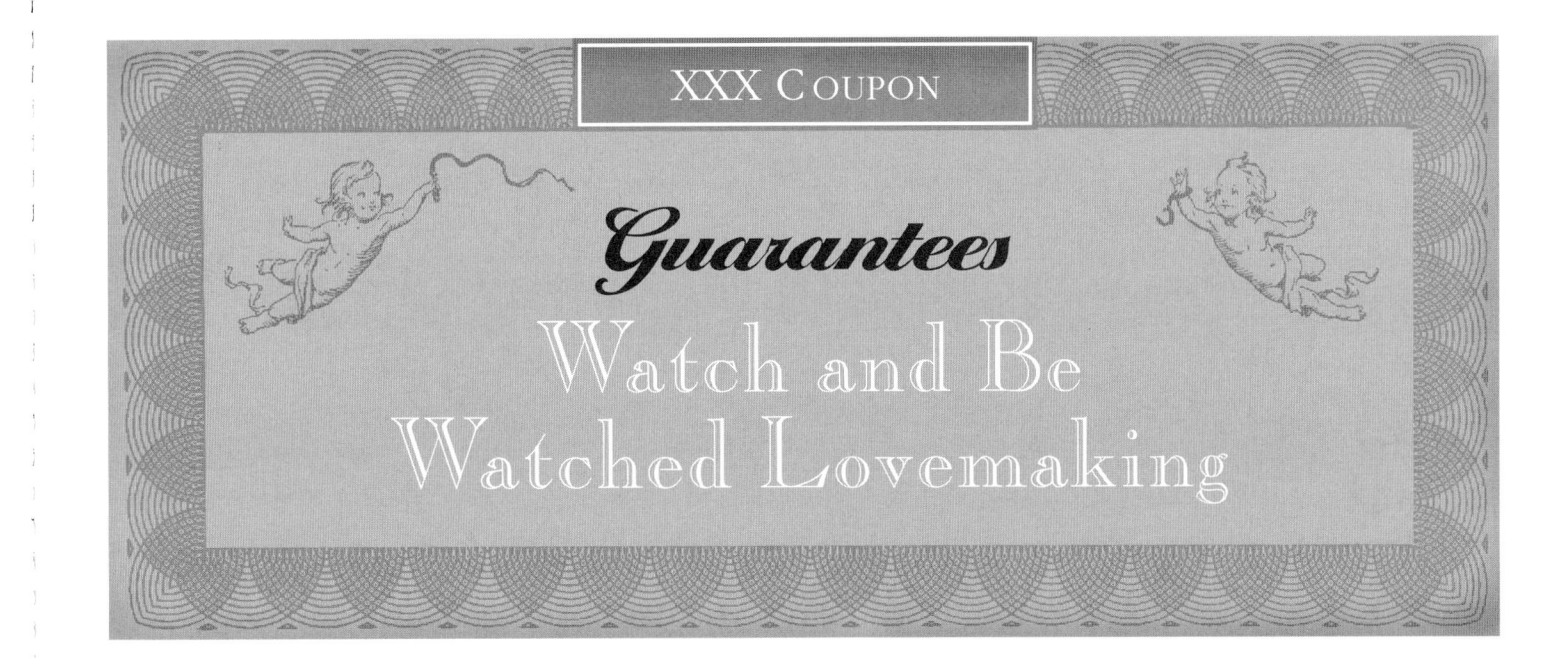

XXX COUPON

Guarantees

Watch and Be Watched Lovemaking

XXX Coupon

Allows Bearer

To Be Hung from the Rafters and Tickled and/or Whipped

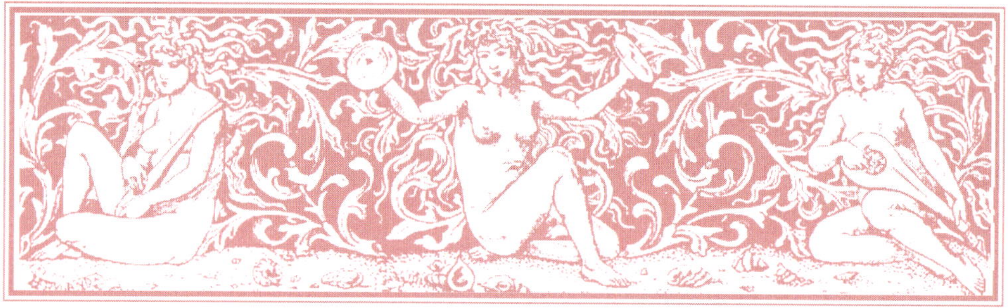

Coupon for Couples

Allows Bearer

ONE

Stay-in-Bed Weekend

XXX Coupon

Allows Bearer

ONE

Mystery Lover Visit

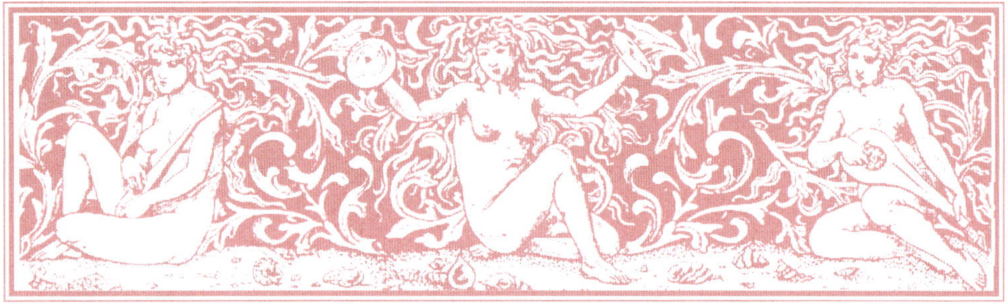

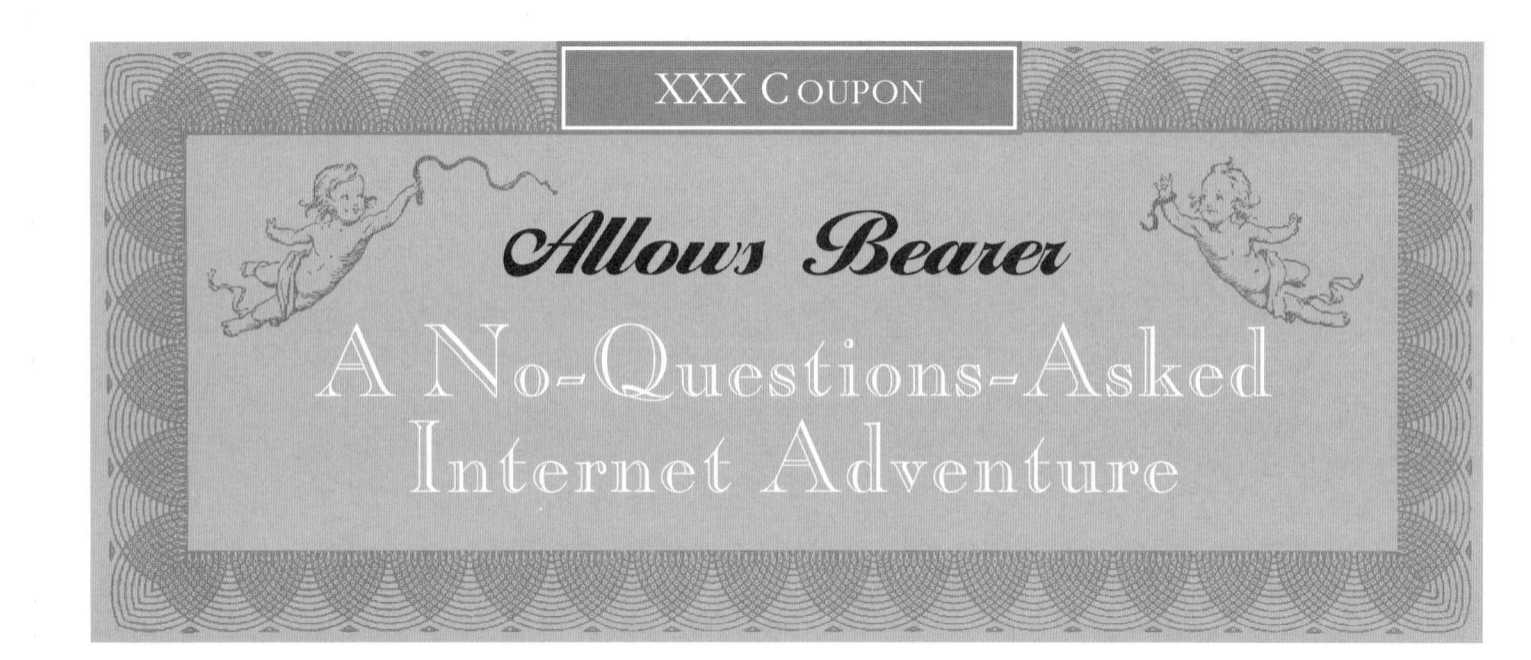

XXX Coupon

Allows Bearer

A No-Questions-Asked Internet Adventure

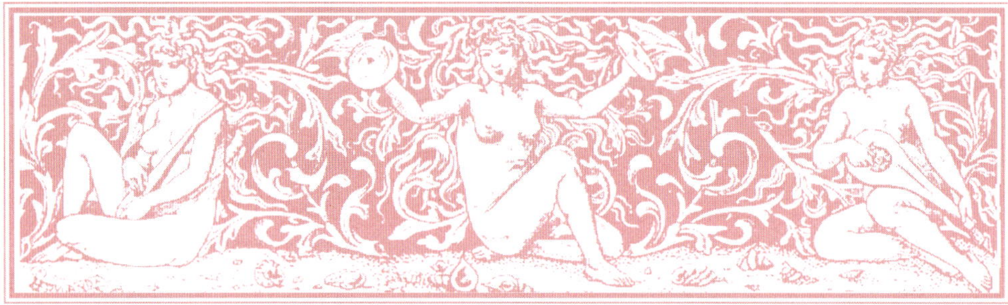

If you have had a particularly wonderful, memorable, or outrageous experience using *Permission Granted* or *More Permission Granted* we'd love to hear from you. And if you've created a coupon you think others might like, we'll consider including it in our next book. Write to us!

Don Byrd and Leanna Wolfe
c/o Longstreet Press
2140 Newmarket Parkway Suite 118
Marietta, Georgia 30067